Will Strong

WAKE

WATCHFUL ALIVE

ALERT

Will Strong

author**HOUSE**®

AuthorHouse™ LLC
1663 Liberty Drive
Bloomington, IN 47403
www.authorhouse.com
Phone: 1-800-839-8640

Published by AuthorHouse   03/12/2014

ISBN: 978-1-4918-5218-7 (sc)
ISBN: 978-1-4918-5219-4 (e)

Library of Congress Control Number: 2014901121

Dedicated to my wife, Betsy Boyd Strong.

Amazing

on
one
misty
morn
i walk i
rub at my
eyes - i'm
open to see
or could it be
the sky sees
me—skywalks
over both land and
the greenblue sea
I talk - with throat's
first thirsting to speak
still wind talks
my ears hear
a ringing conch
shell's spiraling
labyrinth - a siren
singing echoing
more of an ocean
roar - with nothing
ringing too true too

going down

into a Cave
darkly -
or might
be lightly
may say
bravely
Could say
gravely
maybe
ravingly
or plain
ol' going
going onn
way down
deep on a
kind mindsweeping - a
clearing out clouds of yr
doubt
Cave waving off chaos and
blind mindlessness w/ godgiven
focus in locus deep down in self
plunged - streaming dreams of an
uphill flow of water's going blood like
flowing up and flowing down in most
likely Moses style sinai hi desert low d
o
w
into
e
Cave
e
r
deeply
e
e
r
i
n
knowing
o
yet
o
just go down
o
d
o
w
n
s

2

Apprising Sunrise

So this great and wide sea,
Wherein are things creeping
innumerable
Both small and great beasts ...
There is that Leviathan
Whom thou hast made for
The sport of it
                         -Psalm 104

Once I did swim in
a wide open sea
with W. S. Merwin,
Eye'll not see
try, try as I can
a more curiously

hulking skulking Leviathan:
one found in waters boundless
a sea immense ~~~~~~ endless
as well as deep – unfathomably deep
angelically lying, although an angel lost,

an enormous beast curled & tossed
by night's Bible black empty sleep.
Serpentine sea-fright,
a frightful sight all right
slithering and slouching
so creepily crouching
silent –- uncrying

Divinely sported,
heavenly spawned
with one-eye spying
as dreadfully reported
still awaiting the dawn
of sunrisingly bright
brilliant new light.

Taking a Walktalk

I and not I go
       for a walktalk
            together
trying to sort out who is really
      who
  says not I I am the real I
    you know
then again say I come now not I
     it is *I*
     I am the
      one
  I am the one who's here
   to get things done
why not I you don't seem to know
     things
not really now do you not I

   in turn not I says
   you're not one to
    understand
     life
  that very well
  since you know
  way too many
    things
things that in the end
   fail to bring
    deep fun

but says I in return
  I have come to learn
things are true measure
 of what is to treasure
things that I can see
  things that I can touch
   things that pleasure me
    oh so much
things are the real deal
  not those things unseen
    you know what I mean
not those airy fairy imaginings
  that in fact bring nothing
imagine this and imagine that
all caught up in flighty acts of
 imagination

here I am grounded in facts of
        creation
just imagine I am very hungry
    and before me appears a well
        imagined plate plentifully
                filled with fine food
and I ravenously dig into that gracious
    plate awaiting me
            only to find I've been blessed
                    with emptiness

hold on -- wait!
        not I exclaims interjecting
let's say that the plate is filled with
    food that's even better than
            you have in mind
        food delectably divine
    and you wolf down that food
    devouring every last morsel
    then soon you find you're
        hungry all over again
                            my friend
and let's say you pile your house high
        with oh so many things
yet soon you find those many things
        aren't what you're after
            after all
soon you find that more
            isn't really better
        still you keep going after more
                    and more and more
never seeming to get enough of what
            you don't really want
        caught up in an endless taunt of
        things that seem all too important
and once that appears clear enough
        once you know I took the hook
then again you I and not I can go for
    a walktalk together

and I and not I do once again go for a
        walk together
with an azure blue sky to witness those
    cumulus and cirrus clouds

5

SpiritSoul:

it's one's lifefield being
both birthed unto earth
  yet unsoiled and whole
all so concealing but now
  revealing in mystery
flowing through one's living
  and through one's dying
breathing breathlessly
  restlessly peaceful
dreamstreaming along
  floating gently into
that Bible-black sea of stars
  staring into eternity.

Mindfield:

in that endless flowing
  comes that blessed knowing:
one's becoming One with
  the womb-wet sea that is
Mother to you and me.

Here we're in this boundless
  Mindfield of Spiritsoul
found here together to
  live free to be in our
lifefield's flow of birthing
  being breathing growing
learning knowing yearning
  burning finally to
return to our Source of
  course where river (or rêve?)
runs fearlessly, freely
back home - yes, fearlessly,
  freely home to the sea.

Time for One Song

i *am* running out of time come i
to confess not even blinking
an eyelash or say thinking
about just what it'd take
to greyhound bound out
of tick-tock clock's
circle or whatever
shape or pattern
time is so sewn
into of late
since oh ooh
so many of
a tale's
hemm'd
'Once
upon

A

time'
which
could be
switched &
re-stitched:
'Once *below* a
time...'ho hoo -
so, let us flow now
you and I and whoever
should even oddly so
endeavor let us flow now
being perinatally matrixed,
released in Mama Earth's arms
so preter- & free *too* naturally
being birth canal channeled into
new life & crying out once accord's

cut severing chance and opening
to whirling twirling
dervish dance
flinging into flights of
mad gladness
playing on fiddle hey diddle

riddle filled with thrill
of fun *in-fluens-ing* one
to wonder who is there
waiting at that door
& finally opening
up so wanting to
sneak a peek
and finding:

GOD
IS
BEING

that metaphor
for: which wert
& evermore and so
welcome inside thru
that revealing of no
concealing save foolish
pride's second-guessing o'
divine blessing's showing a
knowing of being one with all
kind & shining the Light behind
one's mind

too soon mind blindly winds up wounded
and bleeding dreaded doubts over what
this might be all about & pondering
scene and the unseen & wondering
could we've maybe met *somewhere*
or say somehow prior to *Now?*
and how could what is past
be translated as: *parbleu
deja-vu,* did say you –
ou peut-être vu-jade,
did you say? still
feeling: *ah yes!*
and re-thinking
is *that* **SO:**
that's this
and kiss
is that
and
so

A
kiss is
all there
is - so we
must have met
before awhile
ago in that green
field where dreams
are *all so real* and a
gate open wide leaving
nowhere to hide not even
behind tall fences or those
private pretences which will
speed you to know or sense you
do know since time is blindly yet
ever so kindly running out **Of** s p a c e

why
my   we
are here
now seeing
sans seeing
& hearing *sans*
hearing blessed
thru grace & still
seeking to be the i
of *I* & gazing all too
peacefully with the calm
study of that beguilingly
soulful Mona Lisa like smile

O'

3rd
eye's
spying
so deeply
in one soul
contemplation
praying saying
we need *no* time
only place to pitch
a tent in a mindfully
kind space of fixed and
unmixed attent-ion always
praying that *you need verse*
chanting timelessly into that
one free verse

9

Entering the Circle

Surrendering to the present
Beyond the movement
Beyond the restless
Blessed by stillness

In the Center of the Dance
Space found not by Chance

Past the clouds of clouds
And the shadows of should
Past the bags of oughts
And puddles of thoughts

Free from plots and traps
Mind slips into the Gap ~

Entering the Center
Cause for pause ~

Between the notes
Caesura denotes
That moment fond
Of flowing beyond

Into Golden Silence
Past ideas & violence
Easing into relaxation
Increasing recreation

Through Light and Sound
Discovered ~~ found

Ever so deep
In wakeful sleep

What If

self sure can be one
hell of a clever
whatever to endeavor
to check out now
can't it, spanning it-
self why skyward
enshrouded in clouds
drifting acrOss
draped shape-shifting
taking one form
yet warming to another
somebody embodied
in clOud sifting thru
still willing to
be viewing itself as
well, hell – as
improbably but one self

Odd Evens

even odd
odd even
to believe
in the news'
views - too
pontificated
and leaving
words of
the birds
unheard
and even
uncelebra-
ted - how
odd by God

Mon Dieu – Deux!

it can be too
handy being
ambidextrous
and it can be
far too vexing in
one's electing to
check into one clear
understanding of the
two hands of God or
any other way at say a
weighty sleight of hand

The Circle Dance

"Do *not* do unto others
as You would not have them
Do unto you," Confucius'
Saying sagely advises —
A precept pragmatic, wise.

Or: "Do unto others as you
Would have done unto you,"
So resounds Christ's concept
Unbounded, idealistic precept.

Could it be that Confucius
That ideal would confuse us?
Or else could it be that Jesus
Thot ideal ought to please us?

"As you sow, so shall you reap,"
The Bible & Karma both relate.
Live true and live for keeps —
Staying well aligned & straight.

The Law of Karma would
Have us live as we should:
Actions can bring reward
Done in respect & accord.

Or else actions can harm ya
Done in reaction and discord,
Weighed by the way of Karma.

In time one grows to know
Responses and reactions flow
Naturally- not just by chance
In an All-embracing Circle Dance.

Myth Taken

A grave break

In over reliance

On sheer science

In open defiance of

Mystery & the mythic

Factually, it's myopic

Actually all too mistaken

In its blind myth forsaking.

A Way In

Say ain't chances often easy to
　　be like St. Francis of Assisi
frankly, as easy as it is for soft gentle
　　ocean breezes to ease in motion
in reaching wide open white beaches
　　as easy as it is for clouds to dress
& bless the sky in all its vast nakedness
　　as easy as it is for a furry cat to curl
up in its own world & gently begin to purr
　　as easy as it is for the moon to bloom
& flower in dreamy beams in darkened hours

seems we've hardened to the ease in St. Francis'
　　agenda in surrendering as well as in pardoning
in bending - in mending and in befriending
　　in forgiving for the sake of waking to living
in ceaselessly praying thru increase in playing
　　in a way in comfortably commingling- bringing
out deer without fear - ringing in birds chirping
　　and cooing moving in near - singing in loving
words heard so cheering and so very endearing

What Profits a Man

To gain the whole
                world
Yet have his soul
                hurled
in a hell of greed,
                twirled
beyond his needs.
                A bitch.
Such a magnate -
                so rich
in money & great
                hitched
to a slooow train,
                driving
over time's plain
                arriving
no surprise to his
                demise.

Taking Joy

To
War:
At best
To play a
Game of Chess,
Race for space,
Climb for time.
Scored simpler,
A warped way for
A man to play – why
More a boy taking
Joy in control of the
Whole by breaking,
Even destroying friend's,
Brother's or another's toys

So Being, Being So

why my
i am so
amazed
looking
in to a
maze in
amazing
at first i
see am
and then
i go from
a to z
staring in
to i-n-g
gee, i'm
running
into one
gerund
why my
i'm now
finding
amazing
most a-
mazing
enough
to fly-
my am I
soaring
around
unfazed
unbound
being so
amazed

Say What May

why in the hell be out languishing
    in anguish
when you could as well be wishing
    with relish
in relaxing in latitude of a gracious
    gra-ti-tude
not thinking – not even blinking
    oh, maybe
winking words of thanks for some
    kindmind-
fullness that blesses both alike by
    reminding
no matter any *angst*, just stay open
    say thanks!
mercy buttercups! as French come
    see/ saw it
the garlic to the onion picks thanx
    shallot not
too high bred nor shy hiding a bit
    much grass
could pass as Hispanic if y plant it
    dunka shay
may be germanely Germanic- but
    don't say it
w/ a slow Southern-style drawl of
    thanks y'all!
shay and shame may sound much
    the same &
it ain't any shame claiming thanks
    in any name

Ache Believe

my how
strange
does this
pain re-
arrange
the chambers
of my mind
Feng shui
you
yes i do
enigmatically
explains
this excruciating
migraine
no matter
what vase
or phase
might i
break or
shatter
moving things
around
you won't
quite go
all   to   pieces
in this   messy
process of
clearing things
out
to know
God's being
that measure
of pain
you've come
to gain
which leaves me
to wonder
in mindsight –
is *that* right:
does
ache believe
really
by God
relieve
migraine
through
my gain?

Seeing in the wee Hours

when a 3 a.m. hymn
 begins singing out
is it by any chance a
 chanting or ranting
is it sung solely soul
 enriching - or just
untrustable witching
 hour's bitching - is
it deeply bemusing
 or wildly confusing
is it say teeming w/
 meaning or meanly
fearful - or could it
 be merely a dream
seen unclearly - ah, it's
 all in seeing true
through your eyes with a
 sense of surprise
oblivious to the
 obvious freeing
yourself healthily
 being cheered to
hear clearly enough
 to make sense of
what may seem nothing
 more than nonsense
minted in hints from hours
 seeing wee flowering

23

Gazing or Glazing

one window shows a

gray cloudy sky

one window shows a

clear blue sky

one window shows a

wind blowing

one window shows a

calm stillness

do you know which

window sill

you will turn to –

meaning

to be there leaning on

staring out

unwittingly dazed or glazed

or thrilled

to be window gazing

Riddle of Ridding

a way down

    under in wonder

down, down

    in *duende* as y

may so pray

    God be ridding

no kidding –

    ridding y of God

not even odd

    or even grieving

really relieving

    sinking unthinking

drinking deeply

    steeped in keeping

thirst quenched

    drenching - bursting

into darkness'

    blessings of no

confessings

    or guessings -

just trusting

    in adjusting to

the nature of

    the dark side in

sparking the

    light of what is

more than

    simply right

plunging way

    down under – done in

ways of one's

    wonder in *duende*

On One

Is it a mission

you are on

or - could it be

an act of

commission

spinning in

again so very

sinfully

or is it simply

an act of

ommission

something y're

feeling missing

maybe even

somehow re-miss

in or perhaps

say a slap into

submission

calling for an

act of

contrition

then again

you could give

yourself

permission

& tur'n it into

an active

mission

Addressing Yes

Can it ever be too late
    to tap in & create
to have followed that map
    tracing out the place
for one to be in that zone
    that spot alone- unlike
any other -- really, a sacred
    space one comes to face
in awe - lawfully rightful - an
    entitlement to being free —

fated lateness - one need only
    think of Grandma Moses or
Fyodor Dostoevsky - both in
    their 80's and feeling
great enough to be working
    on masterpieces- can
it ever be late in one's
    creative process—
ever too late to work
    on what one has
grown on the planet
    to dare show
to care to have
    shared out
of generosity
    kindness
mined through
    blessing
addressed in
    one's
creativity
    that
ultimate
    of
yesses

Blame Game

who comes out lamer
in the blame game
whatever the claims
yes who comes out
lamer in attacks so
aimed to defame -
looking back's much
the same whatever
the name & whatever
is claimed still
maims all the same

Hounding Rebound

you might well find in
          unkind unwinding
in putting someone down
          that doubts you come to
put out have a way in turn to
          be found in coming back around
deeply burning in their returning

Circling

and yes odd I see
>   an odyssey
unfolding so boldly
>   in front of me
an odyssey I've oddly
>   seen in a dream
so it seems - a return
>   home grown in my
traveling telling me that
>   all roads do show an
affinity - so it's more
>   circling around after all
a rebounding of *deja- vu-*
>   could that be   *true–*   or
should it be said instead
>   another way - say *vu-jade*
which makes sense of those
>   experiences - to be so naively
believing in them in innocence
>   open – in wonder – in viewing
anew, never having crossed that
>   path after all – wandering freely
or then again – could it be travels
>   tell more a story – recounting from
times past, a story storing yet more
>   questions than answers & calling for
still more of restless traveling on in an
>   odyssey – by God yes – see how odd
chances are it's an endless dancing with
>   a peaceful stillness blessing the center

Wish Delicious

Here's to wishing

               for a name to

claim, one as my

               stick- here's to

fishing out at sea

               for the mystic

waking me in the

               breaking dawn

out spawning mists

               enshrouding

clouds drifting yet

               still shifting in-

to unmistaken and

               unmissed of a

tryst with not if

               uplifting

into a morn born

               unmournful –

evermindful of

               kindness'

blessings as they

               progress in-

to a wish-filled

               mystic thrill

Wishful Mystery

waking to a dream that
seems to be making no
sense – yet its images
are so nettling – so un-
forgetably strange and
unsettling that you drop
pretence and stop your
rationing out rationale
no reason to freeze in
cold icy tricks of logic

you begin in spinning in
changes re-arranging
a view to the true
could it be what you
see in dreaming is
saner tho' not plainer
than in waking since in
dreams life's seen stripped
of superstitions – and
denuded of taboos

unfiltered eying spying
unhesitated creating
an unsealed reality
in a curious sometimes

furious revealing

yet oddly by God con-
cealing the deal leav-
ing a few cards seeable
& others tight-chested - you
seeking to sneak in a peek
to see those close-guarded
cards - not looking to fold
too interested in testing
in calling to see what
the hand might be holding

Airing

Is it really fair
        not to share
or dare or even
        care whether
others fare well
        w/out what you
have come to share

        without spare

Alone – or All One

Is it rude to take to
                    solitude-
not to include others
                    feeling a
need to be alone not
                    retreating
so much as completing
                    oneself in
an interlude – one you'd
                    enter into
later yet deeper - into an
                    inclusion
of others – once that space
                    faced in
solitude steeps into seeing
                    one is in
all – and all is also in one

Magic Moments

It's caesuras we're often not
                    too sure of –
those pauses or gaps friendly
                    to space or to
place – happening to cause
                    breaks in bet-
ween notes devoted to making
                    sound abound
in filling our ears and leaving
                    little room for
resting to hear silence – that
                    respite which
admits in peace from restless
                    questing for
more – ever more to score in

                    our dashing
about doubting, even flouting
                    the sense in
the difference of a dash– yes
                    what blessing
in taking a break – in pausing
                    making room
for a wedding of wonder – that
                    miraculous of
union - one of time and space
                    to take place
set in eternal turning in one's
                    experience of
what now stands in the land of
                    ever-present
time - chimed in the moment
                    heaven-sent
meant for being magically in
                    here and now

Imagining

Is it a mirage or not,
this image, one
imagined there
so daringly between
the ideal – yet
still… dreamed
and what may feel
real - it may be
between – well
between one's self-
esteem & one's
teeming dreams

or say, maybe it's a
mirror image re-
flected in deep
introspection – one
to take a good
look at - not so
much for nitpicking
zits or warts or
anything maybe
short of say seeing
being good plus
the could- given
a healthy self-image
well-imagining I-
deal in the real

The Bringing

hear ideas
        sing flinging - spear it
                fiercely pierces
       3 am hymn howling -
witching hour flowering
          singing shrilly - unsurely
                praying - point
          may be in flinging or in
bringing – can't be   s
         sure - it may be in the tip   p
                of ideas'
         mind's lip sipping a taste   a
too sharp - too piercing for proof   r
            eclipsed by heart's
savoring and favoring – conceiving
            and incubating –
believing and celebrating whatever's
             conceivable and
believable is an image making - waking
            truth   imagined –
dreamed of in that being this's bliss-kissing
               proposing most
surreal of marriages of mind&heart never
            truly apart not now
ideas' feeling reeling real
          don't ask how
            come dreams
         of holy spears
ideas needle
       pointing to *what* i don't know
              why
       just trust sowing - and growing
hear clearly yet
       not say plainly - not that
            spears
       need heed sense sanely
not that spears need yelling to
          point out when
              in singing
         fiercely piercing
flinging shown
       alone bringing
         spears own singing

Thriving Alive

Given to relative living

Driven to live in relation to

Creation either befriending or

Bending to unfriendly unblending

Fix is miXing in trUe through

LiVing & forgiving - thriVing

Alive in knOWing one's

Freed being once seeing

Thru I's eye's true prizing

Wise openness to blessingS of

Yessing w/out 2nd guessing

Shining in unconfined loVe

GiVing & really living

Test in
Less

queasiness
eases in
qualm long
tried in a
quietness-
so deafly
unquestioned
a test in
festering
caught in
fraught
tense &
senseless
shadows
of unknowing
growing
in suspicion
grouted
in self-doubt
not to men
tion mistrust
wishing at
least for
release
hoping for
opening
to peace
as in morn
ing hours of
flowering
empowered
by rest in
no need for
wrestling
w/ questions
no tests in
what is done
and past
at last...

middling

and so here I am in the
                    middle of a phrase –
surely there are ways to
                    bring it to an end - yet
here I am half-way- sus-
                    pended on the 9th floor
stuck on this elevator
                    caught thinking I could
be heading back East at
                    break of dawn when new
stories begin - and then I
                    could find a way to end
this phraSe - but that'd
                    only be a way around
the spot I've gotten my-
                    self caught in here on
the 9th floor which I must
                    not fear finding a way
out of being in the middle
                    waiting for a way out
or at least - a way to end
                    this phraSe -whiCh

raises the queStion of
                    how the phrase even
began -was there a plan
                    or perhaps, it simply
happened in passing as
                    my ego blurts out
I am not your amigo
                    so- where does that
leave me here on the 9th
                    flOor caught in the mid
dle of a phrase with no way
                    up or down. stuck in the

41

middle, a little like a nowhere

        man drinking without

thirst- thinking without

        verse- or worse still

staying haZed in the mid-

        dle of a phrase atonally

stoned on an unending

        lack of resolUtion -

why, smaCks of collUSion

        with J. Alfred Prufrock,

a shy guy who well dread

        knocking at doors-

the dare– the dare -

        who cares to dare

any more - draw the shades

        close the doors - stay

safely cocooned out of the

        way - no telling who's

loOse in the streets - no one

        well worth greeting...ah,

but where's this leading any-

        way -just more stray

wayward dangling thots

        that ought not cross 1's

mind so unkindly- not

        in the midst of muddling

thru puddles of middling

        true piddling in frag-

mented phrasing -run-

        ning on into hints

of sentences executed

        unquestioningly...

trying to get back on

        track thru tonality's

finality -lOSt in winding

        thru the narrow streets

of Istanbul –pulled a-

        long in ceaseleSSSS

Middle Eastern drOning

        endlessly intOning

hey - maybe there's no

        middle since there's no

end to begin with in thiS

        drift ...just then the ele-

vatOr starts to shift

        finally bringing me down

to ground floor- a parenthe-

        ses apparently

eclipsing an ellipsiS

        a seiZUre in the middle

of a phrase - a dark-

        ness at the break

of noon - best I guess

        not to step outside

any tOO sOOn ...

Highly Catifying

Caninonical dogtrines grew too doggymatic over goD for more feeling aligned felinists. A catschism sprung up giving birth to a new kittychism.

Roaming Catolicism was born from this cat schism. The Catolick faith developed the Catacy that rules over all of Catolicism. The Catacy is deemed infallible when speaking *ex catedra*.

A cataclysmic cat fight stirred over whether the Catolick Catacy should rule. Fanglicanism, Whiskeropalianism, Supurranism, Mewthodism, Catism, Catvinism, Purinatanism and still more isms came into being. Yet for all the isms that were created, felinists were finding themselves less and less free, especially in isms like Pentopcatsalism.

More finely feeling felinists realized seeking the Litterall truth was a funlessmental and apathetic approach. So they turned to a cataphatic approach, a way giving paws to reflecting, medtating and catemplating, a more deeply gratifying and highly catifying way to address & to be blessed by the Goddess.

Thanx Too

why in the hell be out languishing
            in anguish
when you could as well be wishing
            with relish
in relaxing in latitude of a gracious
            gra-ti-tude
not thinking – not even blinking
            oh,   maybe
winking words of thanks for some
            kind mind-
fullness that blesses both alike by
            re-minding
no matter any *angst*, just stay open
            say thanx!!
mercy *buttercups* French come see
            or – come
saw it- garlic tO onion picks thanks
            shallot- not
too high bred nor shy hiding a bit
            much *grass*
could pass a, Hispanic(if y plant it)
            drunka say
may be a germanely German way
            donja say it
w/ a slow Southern-style drawl as
            thanks, y'all!

no matter how you may say it,
            in a language may-
be foreign - words of another land
            still from tone
alone you can openly understand a
            voice intoning
words of thanks telling so wellingly
            true starred &
imparted from Deep inside 1's heart

Good Vibrations

any hints of dreaded evil
mental woes long ago in
Medieval times meant time
for the garden – for Good
Earth to pardon coming un-
done, feeling too much heat
coming to drum out of beat
or hum out of tune – foully
scowling - even wildly howling
Caligula-styled - gladly barking
at the moon - darkly stark mad

back to the loving arms of Mother
Earth to uncover the birth of Holy
Communion, wholly coming to union
with earth's naturally nurturing thru
good vibrations, mating life w/life and
re-creating out of kind dirt a washing
away of hurts soiling the mind by
toiling in the garden, a sacred space
to pardon thru Earth's grace, thru
life's vibes flowing in growing of
new life re-newing one's sense
of a holily whole soulful place

now we've come full cycle
in re-cycling the likes of
vibrations running thru
all of creation down to
sparks of quarks photons
light longthronging
to vibrate to wriggle
in neato mosquito
larvae's squiggling
the infinitesimal
essence very
quintessence
of life in its
cellular self

what else *is*

there to share

what more could

Beach Boys teach

than that woOOO

good vibrations

a hymn to acronyming

LOVE as Living On

Vibrational Energy

why it's mingling in the

dingly suchness touching

more than much of life-

good vibes start right

at the very heart of life itself

wealth being Medieval belief in

wellness's swelling up from

vibrations stored&grOunded

there to be found in the core

of Mother Earth's being

Open to freeing us-

trusting in the deepest

essence of love creating

thru vibrating energy

we're urged with and

been blessed to address

ultimate of yesses

to liveliest of

vibrations

The Score

what is it egging
  you on more
to be   begging to
  score-food
is that what you
  are now in
the mood for - or
  yet Is it say
legging out that
  door- what
is it gets yr feet
  wiggling yr
tail wagging yes
  what is it
niggling and just
  nagging y
all the more- yes
  what is it
that makes you
  break out
of one hell of a
  shell- yes
what is It that
  keeps on
egging you on to
  move on-
or to stay on for
  one more
before yr getting
  out of the
door- yes tell me
  just what
is the true scOre

Accorded FOrding

up & down the river we
go looking for a way to
cross over to the other
side - try as we've tried
tho' still we should know
for all of our doubts that
reaching out - that in
entering into interesting
testings is the way of
teaching - of making us
wake into braVing waVes
unspent in the current –
seeing what's meant in
wealth given to living w/
going in floW knoWing
the other side is forded
once we can afford to
get shed of pride like a
snake shaking old skin
jellying along strongly -
smooothly moOOVvving
belly telling - groOOVing
in living through readily
shedding & not steadily
wringingly clinging - in-
stead giving up & living
in dying to trYing to hang
on once knowing it is so
going with that floW of
the unhuShing and on-
gushing riVer - giVer
deliVerer of life

49

Full Circle

How is it that we get
          our wish once we
see in the sea fish as
          Catherine of Siena
as well as sea in the fish
          or again – once we
don't just halt w/ Gestalt's
          Whole's greater than
the sum of its parts yet un-
          folding into the SOUL -
becoming creator in humming
          of its hearts - hardly able
to truly undo, to duly label - to
          control the Whole by trying
to rule by foolishly wishing to pull
          it apart - so tricked in logic
thinking we can pick to pieces the
          One into many & be making
plenty conditioned as by far we are
          in trials of denial in addition
to attrition thru wishing the world were
          found bonded and bound in
pleasingly easy answers - however
          never seems dreamed all that
neatly and sweetly complete - smartly
          charted and graphed – why
what a laugh once we're wise enough
          to realize North and South poles
bring us full circle – with Whole in
          full control - planted on a planet
found round - with no sides to hide or
          take pride in – not in a world so
profoundly well-rounded where airing
          the dare of revolution's grounded

50

in coming full cycle – full orbit in the

astronomical sense bringing

us back around to none other than pro-

gressing to blessings

of rightfully becoming at last

vastly and wholly

one SOUL in the sun

Location - Vocation!

A sense of locus,
one to trust as
one *just* for us - isn't
that what we try
to focus on – where
in the world we
are, where in fact are
we actually in
this splendid galaxy
individually in
one spot - is that all
that we've got
or can we span our-
selves outward
out in the circle to
encompass
more isn't that what
we're here for
extending & ending
up well beyond
one's center – one's
one spot gotten
instead readyand
plotting for more
not timidly limiting one's
self- so set on
spreeeaaadiiing
out more God-
like omnipresence
out beyond
that individual dot

that so certain
center located in
creation-
do we sense some
hesitation – in
accepting just one spot
ungrumbling
in humbling ourselves
growing in one lowly
plot – in tending to
gardening it - or
are we hardened to
smallness in wanting
more all-ness
in reaching
out – in seeking
control outside
one's individual will
the thrill of power
and command in
expanding out
throughout the sphere
cheered on in
domination of cre-
ation by expend-
ing & expecting all
the more glory
is that the sum of man's
fate – just where
to well locate self in

                                    the circle of this
vast universe- are
                        we cursed in the
tension of questioning
                    our place in space
testing ourselves
                        as in a mad race
to the finish line – one
                    we may find finishes
us all in falling for dreams
                        &schemes of crazed
ways of power- bent
                        on extending
out in the circle
                        pretending to be
more than we are
                        at the core of our
single center- one
                        entered - located
right within one's very
                        own soul- made
whole not thru con-
                        trol outside as
tried in pride- yet on
                        the inside where
there is no place in
                        space- nowhere
else in the circle to run
                        or hide - not once
when one enters one's
                        center in that spot
one's got in this vast
                        immensity then
seeing honestly within
                        that dot, that spot
what one's given and
                        what's meant to be

Win-Win with
WN–WN

Waste not– want not!
  a saying pray old & told
repeatedly and reaped in the
  hardest of times – harvested
and sold in not so hottest of times
  in ground downest of times, in best
testingest of kinds & as you may be best
  guessing in tone alone – at first versed in
depressingest of times, a gratingly great fateful
  time well-expressed in: Waste not– want not!
chimed so sublimely in that tersely versed adage and
  abbreviated abruptly into: W n – w n! now whether
you frugally take advantage or instead, you futilely deviate
  from charily & sparingly choosing– you'd well be winning
through faithfully W n- w n- ing – or again, you'd ill be losing
  out, failingly bailing – feeling pressed into presuming there is no
end to consuming, rumbling along bumbling – or else ungrumblingly
  humbling through turning and learning that: Haste not– flaunt not!
is yet another way of pray saying words versed 1st   as Waste not – want not!

Where to Scratch...

is it say a twitch
   more than an itch
is it *really* an itch
   maybe more of a bitch
which bites - lites -
   ignites your wishing to switch

so – which itch is it
   that's got you in a stitch –
getting rich – perhaps
   you're seeing some dumb glitch
getting hitched – then
   again, could it be for getting unhitched
finding your own nitch
   rather than simply swinging at any pitch

my
why
life
can be
full o' ma-
gic or it can
be mildly melo-
dramatic - why it
can be tryingly tra-
gic – it's all your very
own pick naturally - in
scratching right where it
really, really, really itches

Such Stuff

makes one wonder why even
                    wake up only to
end up breaking up a dream
                    turning to schemes
of what seems to be real in
                    the realm of what is
possible – tossed or lost in
                    costs of dealings in a
reality – feeling more like it's
                    possibly but a seamless
dreaming in nothing less than
                    entering in consciousness
and fielding possibilities from
                    what appears simply some-
thing really all too impossible

Embracing

Damn braces. Bless Relaxes.
–William Blake, "Proverbs" from
The Marriage of Heaven & Hell

nagging & unnerving doubts
    seem to come about in

thinking what a drag growing
    old – more & more we

are sold on staying young w/
    our days yet unsung –

much more is in store for us,

    so we trust - in staying
in a way feyly young, maybe

    unpeteringly Peter Pan
of a boyish man rocking on &

    on unstaggering like a

tireless Mick Jagger on a roll

    neVer growing very Old

I heard Hosea once saying in

    a civil rights speech in
Atlanta he preached, you can

    only get old when you
forget how to smile - now that

    line has stayed with me
quite a while - one of those re-
    markable sparks, a gem
of wisdom to treasure in years
    passing – reminding me
to erase bracing fears of aging

    thru relaxing in untaxing
grace of letting a smile find its
    place smartly here in my
heart & embrace it in my face

What Is Up – If Not Down?

ever had one of those up-
side down sort of days
leaving you in a daze
or one of those inside out
yes, an inside Out day
spinning- and again
maybe cursedly reversing
yr way, unsure whether
to stay out in it - or
better yet maybe in out of it
or then again – pouting
doubting over whether
to flat out call it all quits
out checking for directions
twirled in a relative world
facing space w/out grace
of knowing what's up or
down even w/ both
feet planted on the ground

heaven knows those astro-
nauts as they brought us
to confounding up or
down, don't you know, in
hovering over Houston
Space Center unsure
to enter just where they were
way up in the air
up above earth or

down below – could

not be seeming to say which
was so when up or down's
meaning fell in welltelling
where in the hell they were
in creation in relation to
planet Earth very hard
pressed to express in terse
words exactly in fact
where they were hanging out
in the universe

ah but words die hard in our
refusing to excuse ways of
saying phrases like the
sun rises & sets – yet
there's no surprising in the
fact that there's no rising
or setting of the sun, been done
w/ that since Copernicus trusting
adjusting to a heliocentric
cosmos as we now know
sun staying still in its cosmic
station, at least relation to
planet Earth- our words need
a re-birth - a renewal to ring
in new knowledge - need
to check our reflexive thinking
in linking it to what we're
growing into knowing
reflecting & collecting new
ways of saying what in the
world we mean cleanly
the scene doesn't get easy, tho'
when you know the wind, it
doesn't really blow, you
know point of fact actually
sucks – high pressure
suctioning a low growing

into wind— but what the fuck
the wind sucks- now that
is just a bit too mucking
fuch from the very sound of it
must admit it's a strange
strange world that is
unfurling & whirling in winds
of change – it's curtains
on what we feel certain
about even left to doubt what's
up and down – reversing
what we believe in - left
bereft, roaming in misnomers
not readily steady over what's
correctly directed
be it up or down, be it rise
or set, be it blow - or
whatever goes

hear here, how about in
and out – now in and
out – that line fits
motion just fine - the notion
is simple and leaves us no
doubt, the old in and
out – a body moves in
toward a body or out
from it in space –
sure enough cure for any
testy pesky questions on
up and down- and you
could even take care of blown
you know - should you go
more for suck with

any such luck but no need
reading in too much –
the old in and out does
fantastic in getting things
right – getting things so
much better – all the
wetter in splurging that
urge for the orgasmic
experience – one
making good sense of
any sort of a day or a
night to get things right

Oh Those Toes

naughty or good toes
now which of those
do you have – yes
which of those do
you know get to
the point sharply
and smartly – in
pointing out – in
praying – ballet's
way so precisely
& nicely pointed
and poised to
spring swingy
do your thingy
not in simply
gimping along
those bad toes
unflexing flexors
barely excusable
loose toes slow in
not knowing going
untaught & untaut
caught - naughty

Most Likely Cycling

and so in

our mapping

happening

once again

we begin

to expect

we're elect

or select

as the next

to collect

or reject

as say sex

that may vex

lover's hex

ah but heck

who's to check

who connects

into next

once select

or elect

to expect

to begin

once again

happening

in mapping

yet zapping

of gapping

going in

showing in

growing in

one's knowing

Let It Go

why the hell should

           it be held

back– let it rip, not

           just slip

when y're feeling like

           y've really

got it coming on

           come on

don't just squeeze

           it out easily

don't feel like some

           kinda jerk

working at being for-

           sooth so

uncouth - just go

           with it

yes go right ahead w/

           something

Italians idolize

           something

they feel shows you

           loved yr

meal – yes, go ahead

           w/o even a

shred of dread– go

           right ahead

and let that burp

           go urp!

Devil's Fool Take

Slewfoot – *who* foot? Why that

sly Slewfoot

who stews about on feets uneven

and doubles as

Beelzebub, one helluva fella, why

even a Bubba–

hey, could be re-dub(ya)ed Beelze-

bubba the Devil

if you will, causing a hubbub grub-

bing around all

over town just looking to drag you

down, you know

it's so – why that Slewfoot, that

Old Slewfoot

that Beelzebubba, does nothing

but trouble ya

that Satan lurking in churches no

less – so wily

waiting for those supposing to be

chosen feeling

quite righteously well blessed as

God's very best

Telling and Re-Telling

An Original Version:
  Ring around a rosey,
  Pocketful of posies –
  Hiss you! – Hiss you!
  All   fall   down!

A Modern Up-dating:
  Ring around a neurosis,
  Coronary thrombosis –
  Cancer –   Cancer –
  All   fall   down!

And a Re-visioning:
  Ring around a rosary,
  Prayerful like Moses –
  Kiss you! – Kiss you!
  All   rise   up!

Sign-Seeing

not that bad
 sign ad-vice
  sounds nice
   get going -
    signed
    God
      sounds so right -
       get going - God
        and oh so good
        as one should
         be going from
          stuck- numb
           to get going
            growing into
             go in God &
              sounds true
               too even if odd
                like flow in
                 goinGod

And If...

If a paradigm can some-
times shift into a
pair of dimes silver quick
in picking my drift

And if a paradox perhaps
happened to be a
paired ox in being born so
stubborn—doubly
yoked and truly troubling

Well now – how about
meditation – might
it be mediation between
scenes of creation
& non-creation - somehow
coming unbecoming

Poem Is

poem's a kiss of a kind
we come to find in phonetics
poem's a sign of a mind
  heart kindled in kinetics
poem addresses us both
  reader and writer alike
poem blesses us bright
  both in day and in night
poem's a question so posed
  to answers we suppose
poem's an answer also shown
  to questions not even known

poem makes words come alive –
  powers them with overdrive
poem examines extensive,
  turns it into intensive
poem births words into verses,
  begets so they live and give
poem lets words be heard,
  gives so others too can live
poem is a kiss not to miss –
  lips touch in mingly suchness
poem's answer to any question
  and question to any answer
  is simply poem is what it is.

Whiching

It is well-known
&tellingly shown
a poem's found
oh so soundly
and profoundly
grounded and
nailed down in
the details, just
as it's said the
devil's in the de-
tails – or is it in-
stead, God's in
the details - so
what the devil
will that tell us-
is poem known
to have grown
from a diabolic
trick or a divine
mind – which is
it that slickens
or quickens up
what is known
to be a poem

A Humming Coming

best, I guess, for a
poet to confess
to not know it - not
in strict tricks of
logic at any rate -
leave that, say
in a way for others
to cogitate on
creating knowledge
sedulously
studied &educated
in in college
while what seems
so incredulous
in mind's gristmill
grinding- what
seems but wistful
finding little - or
no sense in it – at
least, not those
blind in mental pre-
tension & other
such untouching &
chosen closed
in kinds of defense
yet lets in opens
to those friendly in
starting out from
the heart since there
is where the poets
dare share what it
is they know - it

imparts not simply
answers dancing
more in testing and
interesting kinds
of questions posed
as art's supposed
to start- right where
answers are heard
humming some
where – there
coming & imparted
from the heart

Cure of Heuristics

One thought fills immensity, ... William Blake

Now how to best teach
  is not to expound or preach,
    naturally not scowl or screech

But to devoutly outreach:
  to inspire – light a fire
  of burning desire,

Deep-down yearning
  one fueling learning –
    soaring then returning

To discover yet more
  free once again to soar
    through an open door ~~

Through an apt aperture
  leading to knowledge sure
    of truth's boundless nature

Restlessly wrestling:
  both testing & questing
  re-testing & 2nd guessing

Quickened, aware and free ~
  spirited in Light and in beauty
    living passionately and joyfully.

Eloquence of Silence

come slim stump – speak
yes, you crowned with 3
American flags and standing
some 4 feet tall - plus say
maybe 9 inches more for that
banner
furled
colorful
crown
stump one humble king
w/your cedar gray & tan
sanded skin w/ yr seeing
true thru eyes prizing view
of open auditorium carpeted
charcoalblackbrown w/seats
grass green & pecan shell tan
myriad pews of church upright
chairs w/aisles mazemaking la-
byrinthine between close woven
rightight knitfit seating- do come
stump- what greeting have you
for an audience so huge– so im-
measurably immense – yet so
hushed as rushes of marsh there
before you – not any words harsh
no - one wouldn't dream you'd ever
launch into chauvinistic flaunt or
say rattle patriotic prattle – pray no
gain in saying words fatally chaotic
ideologically idiotic or quizzically quix-
otic – come stump, what *is* your style
with red and white stripes branded
so loud & with those stars so proud
what *are* you saying- voiced in words
so choice - yet without even a voice
gee be Shown perhaps an attempt
at that *per*fect expression of con-
tempt - silence... or could it be some
a fugue - or refuge in subterfuge
this deep down profound
soundlessness of yours this
poised contemplative quiet
of yours – could it be some
meditation or a reflection
on tranquility, on beauty of
stillness – that gliding
gracefully calm of a duck
above water - yet be-
low go feet furiously
paddling – belying
below – the *dance*
still goes on not
by chance but
by kind design
of on-flowing wave of creation
life washing
in - out - in

what *are* you telling us in
words unvoiced   stranded
as you are awash in a sea
of change   what is it you
see in waters swirling &
eddying re-arranging &
ever changing estuarine
scene seen moving & re-
moving things – nothing met set – yet there you are stump standing with
3 flags crowning/clowning(?) your head – there you are unplanted from miles a-
way transplanted there baring witness to winding creeks speaking only of change
of waves of change – of a swirling world of change – how strange that life rests in
change – how *very* strange – sounds from a dream it seems – nature *resting* in change
and your silence *speaks* to us -
your silence speaks w/o violence
your silence makes ultimate sense
of a world whirled ever in motion
since your silence speaks out of un-
spoken unbrokeness welling up from
depths of God's speaking in silence
holding no pretence no parades &
no charades no shocks from showy
mocks of flags tagged on flashy rags
designed to divide   to take sides to
claim fame & glory - when you stump
you've come to know in quiet humble
ways   that silence tells the real story
w/ a sense of eloquence a sense well
beyond ideas unclear and founded in
fear beyond ideas setting boundaries
and founding settlements bound in
burden of stones of law cemented &
set in obsession w/possession beyond
those supposed closed defined confines
of time & space & opening to a theology
of *gee*-ology – time passing in passion
of flowing & going changing and re-
arranging what *is* – and what is to be
all in its own course – all from 1 source
rooted in depths of flowing and born in
breath of going - yes *going* w/ flowing
in ultimate knowing – *being* is freeing

All-American Girl

look at her there
by the book display
red & white stripes on
front of her sweater
flag on her bag
black elevator shoes
skintight jeans
pouched out bottom
buns she's gottum
blond hair coiffed
just below black cowgirl hat
topping it all off
she's an all-American
righteously styled child
flag bosomed
flag bagged
levi-jeaned
cowgirl capped
all-American girl
yes she is
gee whiz
so she is

Adage a Dog's Way or The Min Pin Spin

pirouetting you bet, getting
    a new leash on life for a
        dog   staying at bay -
lounging yet longing seems *blasé*
    lying while laying, some possum
        play resting - yet expecting
so faithfully   waiting and praying — say
    in abeyance w/ prayerful paws - paused
        sensing a scent, a hint of *walk* on
the way - with ears hearing, tails telling and
    heart smelling a move —about to start out
        the door— *now* is that *prima* temps - that
prime time for a romp - *more* than ready to pounce and
    bounce - to keep leaping and bounding all set to
pirouette, to spin round and round *adagé,* a dog's way
    at ballet - but no going slow tho' chapping to
échappé or is it *jèté* one's self — oh what the
    hell, just jetting out the door— enough of
        staying too damn stuffed *en dédans*
now's time for going *en* dehors out the door
    of course! time to get going no time
        to talk and to balk at walking
now *is* time for *pas* de *chien,* my friend
    enough of that *pas de chat,* as a
        matter of fact - *now* is
time for dogs' ballet you may say -

out fast at last —good *galops* galore!
    replete- with play of *petit jètés*
        no begging to begin at *beguine*
or some such dance scene elevated *w/relevé*
    relievingly leg lifting positions shift-
ing *a la* second - dans *la* second - save for les
    chien avec pliés de *pissée* which so imposes
        pose w/ no quickie *des* partes from *demi*
piées or *squatie-piées* (be it he or she respectively)

still more ardent testing comes from arabesquing
        way too *penchée* - too much dare egging on
                two legging *en l'air*- hardly fair
yet no way to miss w/ *glissé going* gliding
        over yard after yard searching hard
                for just *the right* spot to
pas de poopée tho' some may say it's
        boors' way - leaving plops of
                poopée for others to make
their way   thru unkindly mined fields
        never minding how they might feel
                yet the dance goes on- with
no decreasing Dionysian revelry with all
        that devilry spouting out urine and
                sprouting piles of dung all done
in delight of dumping and prancing enlightened
        panting in sweet heat dancing to pounding
                beats of dogs' nimble feet in bounding
over immaculately manicured and chemically manured
        yards - over streets of asphalt and sidewalks
                of concrete – the dance goes on on floors
soft & hard on stages narrow & long or open and wide
        dogs having nothing to hide – their chance to
                dance– their chance to take people to a
performance w/ no need reversing to rehearsing for
        a dog's way of dancing *adagé* a no-going
                so slow show–done in full display

Thriving on Jiving

So how 'bout dem divers
They just thrive on jive.
They're slick pickers
of bumper stickers:
Divers do it deeper
Stay down longer
Come up wetter
Always satisfied!

My, why jeepers!
They do it deeper.
They go in stronger
and stay down longer.
Say they come up wetter,
Why, what's even better—
Yes, they're always satisfied,
Many fathoms deep in self-pride.

Why Sit and Wait?

If couples can come
    to copulate,
Who'd knock socks
    that sockulate
Or those rockin' jocks
    that jockulate
As well as undies
    which undie-late?

Not remote for coats
    to coatulate —
Or unusual for shoes
    to shoesulate.
True for blues artists
    to bluesulate.

It swings for singers
    to singulate,
Rolls for soul artists
    to soululate.
Must be that Yogis
    yogulate
Gosh, philosophers
    cogulate.

Looks like book writers
    bookulate -
You know it, poets
    coupletulate.

Great- why sit and wait
    to create-amate!

OPEN TEST

EVEREST
NEVEREST
DESERVAREST
EVERNEST
WEATHERBEST
DRIVENEST
DIVEST
SHIVEREST
EVERTEST
MEASUREBEST
EVERATTEST
OVERTEST
SEVEREST
PERSEVEREST
TAKAREST
DIVERTEST
CLEVEREST
AMUSINEST
SWERVINEST
NERVIEST
INNERTEST
COVERTEST
INNEREST
INTENTEREST
ERNEST
ATTENTAREST
ATTESTBEST
INVESTEREST
ENDEAVORBEST
EARNAREST
INVESTAREST
TREASUREST
CONSERVEREST
PRESERVEREST
ABUNDAREST
REVERREREST
RIVERREREST
SWIRLEREST
DERVISHEREST
GIVEREST
LIVINBEST
EVERBLEST

Encompassing All

Of course – a compass, that's what we need
    to point us to love –
love's compass, yes that's the one to lead
    us along the path above
however, there is room to wonder –
    what position's passion on love's compass
do we fashion compassion when love comes to pass
    or do we freely take aim
and hit on fantasy or fame
    gamely we'd come chancing fantasy
 namely not fame, shan't we see?

Say, where the hell's this thing called Love anyway –
    here, let's check for directions
even if we're cleft, bereft with rejections:

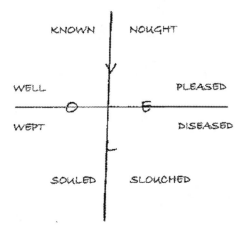

So which way, which way did you say –
    Said directions seem much too askew
which way - really I must ask you
    love seems to point every which way –

switching North Star KNOWN deep down SOULED,
    seizingly PLEASED to swellingly WELL, so I'm told
then too, KNOWN has shown NOUGHT even when it ought
    and wholly SOULED can grow grouchily SLOUCHED
not to mention feelings that PLEASE can breed DISEASE
    and what seems to go so WELL can well be also WEPT

    Still I need a needle true pointing like a star
        one to let me know where I'm heading –
    why it's my head I'm losing, so I'm dreading
        here's my heart I'm choosing, so I can re-start
    kindly bring me a compass, the compassionate kind
        so I don't come passively to lose my mind –

    My clingdom for a course,
        one encompassing compassion
    lest nocling'd come pass along
        nocling of course save remorse.

An Amazed Gaze

and it's there in Istanbul
where this red-head in a
skin-tight dress stands &
fully gazes at me in my
cut-off jeans & in a shrill
trill of sheer incredulity
she shrieks out loudly–
and whoOO are you?!
why my, my, my - I'm so
surprised &dumbfounded
that I can't seem to openly
claim my very own name

so I keep on up the steep
hill to the Hilton just too
stunned to even stutter or
mutter out who I am - so
jammed am I by her pie-
eyed staring in her cherry
red dress - glaring hard
enough to even undress me
then ah - that cry whoOO
are you?! swept me into
silent stammering - left me
but to wink w/out thinking
therefore, am I? well hell
I didn't score w/that whore
busty looker of a hooker
gazing, amazed at bare
legs egging her into that
richly pitched outcry
one so stunning in that
moment it switched me into
unbroken silence, unspoken
in anonymitynot all
too sure whoO I might be

85

Especially or Speciously

prim   all cotton   medium blue sweatshirt she
   wears with such   azure   sky assuredness
as she distances   herself well   over to one
   side & cockpit closes herself into a book
a delicate gold crucifix   next to her chest
   dogtag style over bold white lettering
COLUMBIA THEOLOGICAL UNIVERSITY
and the jeans, pale blue jeans they fit
   snugly with a smart English cut just
above sockless feet pressed in those
   so fashionably brown Oxford shoes
petite — barely 5 feet standing on toes
   topped with short hair, dull blond and
cropped manly close bowl-like yet layered
   ever so subtly betraying a slight hint of
woman and framing in a deeply intent frown
   studiously homed down on so thick a tome

the *look* apt look of intent contemplation
   befitting a rapt vocation of one so truly
   devout – that dear deep look of near
   meditation   shutting out all others
   around her religiously pure & her
   so academically sure self why
   who would dare to interrupt
   her in well-styled affinity
   for the study of divinity
   why - only a spider' d
   dare to sit down be-
   side her to check
   what the sweet
   petit's hording
   & lording in
   so holy a
   bowl

Dixie Tricky

Cold a bitter cold day
in February to be out
hitch hiking a ride
with wind whipping
chill even through
my leather jacket
cars whizzing past
fast & chilling air
still lower   w/ cars
whisking on by briskly
speeds unheeding other
than cars at speeds not
blinking or say not even

thinking about anybody out
in hard biting cold about
whether to take time to
pull over - whether to
take a risk & pick up
a stranger to take a
chance on a hitch-
hiker not so likely
these days not w/
reports of oh so
many *happenings*
nowadays- just
no way of know-
ing *what* you'd
be in for picking
up some hitchhiker
a complete stranger

hold on now - that's *me* i'm
talking about that's *me* out
here in the cold that's *me*
stuck out here thumb held
high hoping looking for
a ride watching far *far*
too many 1 person cars
zipping by my *my* look
at those American flag
decals with the slogans
scribed over UNITED yes
UNITED - wonder what that
means - maybe *U're Not In
This 'Ere Drive* must be it
no shit *Eat-My-Dust* sticker
style & rebel flags - oh hell

    yes rebel flags - hold on now
    Con-fed-erate flags this is
the South is it not land of
    hospitality - hell yes it
    is - land of hospitality
    here i am still chilling
    in the land of Southern
    hospi-tality Sucha-run
    Sloth-erun Sloucharun
    Scofferin hospitality
    who'd believe a land so
    hospitable would dare be
    leaving you out in cold
    so long standing out in a
    freezing cold no not in the
    friendlily sunny Southland
    is how-spit-able more like it
    or how 'bout howspitabull hmmm

    zooming by they go with no time
    and no reason - hush my mouth
    not here in the South love it
    or get yr ass out words once
    rifled by Skynard at Young -
    remember Southern man don't
    need no critics pickin' on
    how he's gotten - why he
    is fine shining on as
    a good old boy - oh boy
    i'd sure love a ride
    now   as I was saying
    anyhow this here is
    the South the grand
    land of hospitality
    why truck's pulling
    over for me - a black
    man's giving me a ride
    so much for those good
    old boys whippin' by in
    style w/ leather inside &
    shiny outside trucks with
    rebel and U. S. flags stuck
    side by side -- here is one
    dented in & smashed out vent
    window pickup stopping for me
    someone knowing what being left
    out in the cold's about- i am so
    thankful to get out of the cold -
    brother am i glad to catch a ride
    way down South in the land of hos-
    pitality long forgotten look a-way
    make your way in Dixieee Land - ain't
    the South just grand - yes ain't it so

Rap Trap

carpet's fault you know
shows all those crumbs
that   left-over hash
every bit of trash
little bits of what
collects - rejects
flecked on floor
carpet it shines
picking up left-
behinds carpet's
how old now - been
one good carpet yes
you bet - yet all
the same carpet's
one to blame for a
mess   scattered out
mess spread out and
left behind - yes the
mess left - one that
could   be called
colliteral damage
or could be tapped
as friendly fire or
could just be bagged
as carpet's luck in
getting struck w/ some-
one's unconfessed messes
& left taking messages
yet - carpet's one to
lay blame on harping
&carping on the fact
that carpet is one
unflattered drmat
unmindfully & so
matter-of-factly
splattered with
all kinds of
crap crashing
a rash of true
trashing w/ no
missing mashing
down what's found
grounddown into nap
tactfully taking a
raking tho' sometimes
sucked up to yet mostly
ragged & tagged- trapped
into taking unkind raps

Dredge Hedging

Hot coffee –   aaaah – *hot coffeee*
   c'est café chaud noir
the French say it with such savoir
in Spanish you could again say
   café negro caliente
whichever way you may call it, a
   black coffee café noir or café negro
which oily or lean bean did indeed grow
   picked far away maybe say in Arabia
or closer to us reaped at Costa Rica
   could've been culled more under in Columbia
or carried maybe even from the Caribbean
   just making it from Jamaica
could've gotten mailed from Guatemala
   or have been sailed in from Venezuela
wherever these beans were seen
   sprouted and routed from,
   toasted and roasted at
now this silty brew comes filtering thru true
   to pursed lips softly smacking up that welcome
steamy black intrepid intruder who'd enter near
   urbanely easing in smoozing in unctuously
ever so sweetly like skim thin oozing molasses sy

                              r
ah – but in fact it's the nose first knows   u
   well before the lips take that first sip   p
to slake that cursed thirst – yes olfactory   p
   nerves serve first notice of coffee in its   p
offering up its own distinct aroma   p
   often smelled, one well its own   p
why you don't even have to think   p
   with coffee that odor's clearly known   p
and that taste – again coffee's got a flavor   p
   unmistakable (to match one's unslakable thirst) p
a flavor one soon learns to savor,   p
   one learns to like much like Scotch   p
an acquired taste – sipped & slipped into   p
   a nip here, a nip there   p
mixed w/ water or soda or neat, cold or – p
   well, i *do* declare –   p
surely not *hot* Scotch,   p
   scotch that botched thought   p
dropping Scotch and hopping   p
            back   ppppppppppppppppppppp

to coffee –
   it's hard not to like good coffee
good steamy piping hot coffee
   what a shot it's got, what a shot
such a sure surge, caffeine urged on
   in spite of its own bitter bite,
bitter even below sugary cloaks
   and behind milky masks, those
clever endeavors to try to disguise
   that iniquitous liquid's bitterness
yes, in spite of that inevitable taste
   one we love to make haste
for – hard not to grab a cup hooked
   once just a few you took, just enough
to obligingly blink - why my am i getting
   high plied wide *awake* simply
sitting here sipping on this wonderful drink

cold coffee – *hmmm* – how cold
   has to be boldly *cold*
chilled nicely with ice
   or it turns kind of ukky yuk
cooled to a lukewarm cup
   of nastily unmasked muck
now it's rough enough to
   make you up and chuck,
enough to make you come and
   puke that bitterly biting
lukewarm not tasting near right
   cup of barely warm coffee
enough to make you think –
   is *this* what i wake to
    is *this* what i shake to
     hurry up slip to my lips
      and quickly get a sip
better be hot *hot* or at least cold *cold*
   but to come out *luke*warm – gag!
what an absolute drag!
   can coffee *really* be that bad
    lukewarm, puke born
     be *hot* – or be *cold*
but that in between scene –
   neither one nor the other, brother
    that *comme çi,* comme ça
   hardly held hot & can't claim cold
    um coffee – cough ah
     oh sister – oh bro*ther*
    ah *misses* – oh mis*ter*

somewhere stuck   in between
sure can become a drag
not going one way or the other
not having any *real* druthers
caught in between the hedges
left way high up on a ledge
and feeling this can't be *it* —

not this Wagon Train overstrained brew
not this ill-famed cup of dirty pisswater
not this not hot and this not bold
not even   shockingly cold
*luke*warm   puke foam
cup i'm drinking from
no doubt just must
for Chrissake spit

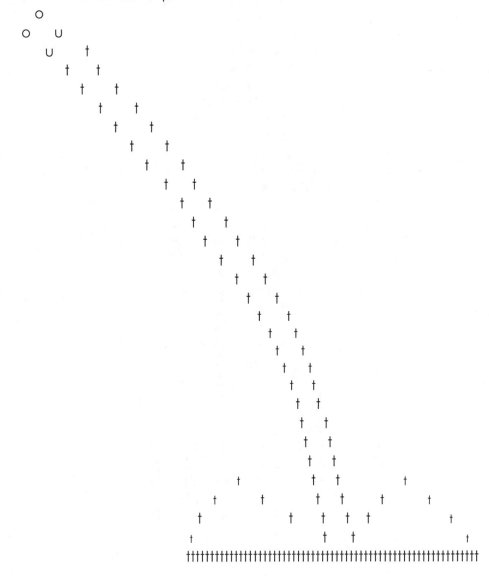

Feline Fine

a feline state of mind

                laying lazily supine

feeling great – well–

                say feelin' so fine

yes – in that fe-line

                state of mind, one

created really as one

                as a matter of fact

superior, so explained

                Mark Twain – one

intriguingly interior

                and independently

insouciant - why even

                defiantly self-

reliant and undyingly

                most mystifying

without even

                blindly trying

wise eyes fairly

                clairvoyant

and chatoyantly

                haunting – softly

sauntering through

but *one* of nine

lively thriving

on the ease of

self-pleasing

w/o even a telling

trace of any

hellish teasing

When it's hard and when it's far easiest

Wizards are ones of
course who don't find it
hard to openly play
in having their own way.

Wizardesses, as one
would well guess, address
things gamely in the
same way keeping to deep

play laughing strong
along the pathway to that
wonderfilled Land of
Om where once one winds

up there, one under-
stands that land's not so
grounded down yet in
stead comes from a sense

of fun - from wisdom
of the heart's starting out
free from doubts in a
land full of wonder, that

amazing land where
mind finds soul's wholeness
embodied in & blessed
by flesh's, by physique's

breathing life into the
mystique of being free in
seeing true through
the eyes- soul's yoking

spoken in wholly come
unioning body&soul found &
sounded in the heart's
homing in *prana* through
zoning in chant planted
in wizardry's wisdom coming
to   humming   that on-going
ever-growing oooOOOmmmmmmm

Involving
Revolving

pumping the prime
rhyming the jump
stumping the time
grinding the grump
bumping the blind
denying the grumble
tumbling the pile
gliding the glum
thumbing the wild
sliding the slump
dumping the whine
climbing the hump
lumping the pine
subliming the stumble
crumbling the crime
frying the frump
trumping the tried
unwinding the clump
dumping the jive
kniving the numb
humbling the pride
resigning the dumb
drumming the dried
widening the wonder
plumbing the mind
mining the fecund
thundering the shine
divining the plum
summoning the kind
reminding the sum
funning the find
priming the pun

Rearranging Changes

towed into slowed mellowness

gulled into dulled sullenness

clad in a shabby drabness

torn in forlorn mournfulness

hitched in a pitched bitchiness

jabbed into a grabby crabbiness

brushed into a husky brusqueness

rushed into hushed untrustiness

flashed into a crass brashness

deployed in annoyed coiledness

speeded into heedless greediness

heated into a fiendish meanness

fumed into a rude crudeness

boiled into foiled spoiledness

zapped into a trapped madness

greeted in seeded sweetness

re-styled in unbeguiling smiliness

mended into blended friendliness

wrapped into a happy gladness

gloved in one covering lovingness

dressed in blessed forgiveness

entered in engendering tenderness

shown in a glowing knowingness

Song Sung True

Whoa now! How so –
how's it we know
we must have joy and
woe as thru this
world we go – drat, is
that *true* - joy and
woe *too* - could Blake
so*mehOW've*
ma*de a m*istake...?

How about staying well
wedded to ecs*t*asy
happy & fre*e* - spinning
der*viSh*ly like R*u*m*i*
dancing a walz o' *wit*
hymn singing to the
land an*d* the sea like
one Walt Whitman
be*aming* & ch*anti*ng
being che*er* n*OW*
like Baba R*a*m D*aas*

How about crowding out
loud mo*men*ts of
doub*t* – of w*O*e lik*e* the
busy b*ee* who has
no ti*m*e for s*orrOW* -
d*izz*y bu*sy* be*es*
we would be if we could
dr*OW*n *out sad*
s*oun*ds – if we could
get th*ru* with*out*
fe*elin'* th*ose* bl*ues*

98

Not that we need to
chOOse those deep
down blueS - those reAl
feelin's find a way
in their own say Sliding
on inside – creEP-
ing in – stealING in on
soft cat's feet seeking
in darkness w/ haunTING
chatOYAnt eYes in
pEERing into shadOWs
knoWINg there is a
way thrU – thrU the
blUEs gettIN' on
down in it – feelING IT –
thrU & trUE since
blUEs is a feeLIN'
to bE deALIN' in –
blUEs reVIEws and
sINgs trUE tOO
a soNg suNg trUE to
be gettIN' reAL in

Would You Be So Kind

not to confuse ya

with news of

my blues and not

to diffuse what

I'm feeling as un-

true - but I've

got to ask ya

w/o any mask

sure, y could laugh

or simply flat

out refuse – still

yes, I will go

ahead - electing

to ck - hoping

y'd not reject even

tho' y don't know

what to expect

would you be

so kind – would

you mind say

serving as my

very own muse

Unshown yet Known

Oh my, oh what is it I know –
like Columbus sailing away
verily in search of mainly aloe
vera - and other things nice
that we're more aware of like
of course gold and spices
sailing long bright days & into
infinity enlightening nights
going on & on & on braving
wave after wave after wave
knowing in his going – in his
sailing on, there would be
no failing – wealth's bound
to be found in the journeying
out on the open sea, out there
in the salt air – daring to be
seeking, dreaming into seeing
what surely he knows awaits
him, what baits him on for the
known unfolding into shown

unshown to known - known to
shown - chancing thru one's
dancing with what feels could
well be real – not hesitating
or waiting for fate to create yet
steadily ready to move on in
groove - growing in flowing
going with the known as if
it is not just discovered but re-
covered as one's very own

Turning Journal

skin turned open journal
   with needles turning out
pictures of time past - of time
   painted to stand fast through
pictures at hand - at arms flexing
   on biceps & triceps – resting on
chests pecking pectorals major and
   minor gripping nipples w/ uncryptic
scripts of hot/cold-sweet/sour-chocolate
   & vanilla - flavors to thrill ya – words &
pictures to be sure on backs on necks on
   butts on what the heck - even on genitals
getting it all and whatever's left of the rest
   on legs begging for it up high on thighs
or going low around ankles – pictures
   hanging - at any conceivable dangle
and any *un*believable angle framing
   time aiming to treasure pleasure
and to re-endure pain – yes, pain
   again &again &again &again &

an instant replay – re-seeable
   reviewable - a ready review
i d marker too – that tattling
   tattoo signed/designed in
ink's sinking in - inscribing
   & describing in indelibly
telling style   surprisingly
   metamorpho-sizing –
reshaping - rolling trolls
   into dolls - & making
vines snakes winding
   around firey hearts
flaming red hot with
   desire clear clues
tattoos blazing and
mamazing pictures
tinted hints unhidden
   in hues - in scrolling
rolls beholding angels'
   wings curls and swirls
unfolding to *los Diablos'*
   diabolical twirls flaming
dragon's wild wrath while

acclaiming crossed and lost paths
flaunting fantasies' wishful twists &
   wants & taunting histories' once
missed trystful unrequited haunts

in skin's journal - in skin's way
   of spurning propriety – and
heaving sobriety leaving be-
   hind society's circles with
curtains drawn - gone - no
   more game played staid
cast in new roles - in new
   folds - making up new
parts undaunted by any
   unchosen aunts and
   avuncular of skunks–
   coming out far from
debutante balls – and
   suave soirees, need-
less to say - coming out
   in colorfulest of classes'
clashing – crashing party
   lines and feeling just fine
departing letting roundest of
   farts fly – soundly breaking
class barriers – out choosing
nouveaux nous - dusting off
   fussiest and yuppiest of yahoos
   tattoos do well battle - defining
lines finding its own kind - rattling
   too familiar of family & precisely
nice relatives to boot - who dares to
   tattoo skin (human leather) – who
cares to be sketched & etched – who
   fares to flock together fondly bonding
into one of most atavistic and mystic of
   brother & sister-hoods – unflinching &
unsquirming at needles – determined to
   self-canvas and self-affirm – fleshing out
in skin a portraiture – a yearning to journal
   to be sure of what once was and to picture
what one wants to be - as well as telling one's
   identity – pointed out in skin's turning journal
through choosing reviews - in one's own tattoos

Such a Sweet Smile

for real evil
what you do is
       conceal –
             hide away:
               you play hide
                        and seek
so to speak
isn't that your game
   why not come
            out evil
     come out if you will
       and play
             with no shame
                    in the light of day
why there you are
   not really so slack
             laying back
   not so very far away
             in those shadows
you've grown to know
    all too well
realizing of course you've got
    nothing to sell
just hanging out
           lurking around
      the corner
            looking to turn things
           upside
               down
           or inside   out
yes you juke and you jive
         and you do thrive on doubt
rambling and scrambling yourself
       evil into *live*
      even past tensing
      devil into *lived*
now who's there to forgive
   your many outrageous reversals
   and your well-staged rehearsal

all directed with bent intent
toward perfectly performed
and unreformed
misdirection –
or is it rejection
or then again crafty creation of
misinformation
oh evil one
it never seems to fail:
you come so cleverly costumed
too often awfully well dressed
leaving no one to even guess
you're any less than a gentleman
or say a gentle woman
as one would naturally presume
my why you're so chicly
so surprisingly disguised
behind that sleek *veil*
of a glad hand and
a beguilingly sweet smile
a touchingly sweet smile
yes such a sweet sweet smile of
complete deceit.
Now oh evil one there you went
and created your very own religion
the religion of just One Commandment:
Not to grin is a sin!
why *Mon Dieu,* is it true too that you've
translated your own Bible in your
inimitably inimical style:
"In the begrinning was such a sweet smile..."
come now what *is* the deal
oh evil one
Est-ce possible —
could you *possibly* be for real?

Heard in
Words

Crazy ways some
words come
to spill out thrill as
well as
spell out hell and
can even
lead you into be-
lieving in
bleeding- needing
forlorn
mourning and
grieving

Weirdly searing
when words
end in myStery
despite
tight simplicity
spun and
done in Kafka-
esque style
arabesque in
best guile

Painfully plain
words gain
in intensity cut
sorta short
set in brevity
adroit-
well pointed in
report

Cheerfully clear
words are
after laughter
oddly
juxtaposed
not as
supposed - so
heavy
yet lightened
when said
in levity-
haw hee

and churningly
words turn
dreams' cream
from reel
flutter whipped
up to utterly
real feelings

About the Author

Long have I loved writing: I loved writing letters in my younger years; I felt I expressed my feelings better through writing. This collection of poems represents some two years of focusing on writing just poems. Poems about whatever came to mind, no matter how simple it may have seemed.

For a while I got stuck on writing politically connected poems. I even put together a chapbook collection entitled: "Bush League Fatigue." But after several months of that political focus, my mind grew too fatigued over politricks. I realized I needed to return to more creative writing.

My earlier years were spent on the road. After cramming about 3 years of college hours into 2, I burned out on college life and opted to join VISTA, the volunteer domestic peace corps. That took me to Albuquerque and later to Houston. After that I travelled on to California: to San Francisco and "Bezerkely" where I lived for about a year. Then I motorcycled back East to Savannah. I felt the urge for more travelling.

So I flew over to Europe and hitchhiked my way through 24 countries, getting as far East as Istanbul. I'd been awaiting a check from the government for my time in VISTA, but it never came through. Travel funds almost depleted, I headed Westward, hoping to find my government check at one Embassy after another. I somehow managed to make it to Lisbon on just $10.00, an odyssey worthy of a book in itself.

Back in the U. S. A., I soon felt that travel urge again, this time heading from Savannah to Washington D.C. I found work in a office polling folks about whether we should withdraw from the Vietnam War. Once Nixon was re-elected though, the office was closed down. So once again I felt the call to head Westward Ho! Which is just what I did: I packed up my VW van tagged Picadilly Van Go, painted all over the way it was, and I drove Westward with a couple of others. I ended up in Venice Beach later moving to Santa Monica and then to the Echo Park area of Los Angeles.

I found work as a cook at Formerly a Well Known Restaurant as well as a writer for "People's World," the West coast version of "The Daily Worker." Earlier years on the East Coast I'd edited and written for a couple of underground papers. First I'd worked on "The Great Speckled Bird," reviewing music events, concerts for groups like Pink Floyd, the Allman Brothers and Grateful Dead. When I moved back to Savannah for a while, I started up "Albion's Voice" using Armstrong State College's Literary Club money to get it started. "Albion's Voice," the name taken from William Blake's giant Albion, survived 6 issues, the last of which was tagged: The First Annual Save the World Issue, filled with loads of good graphics I'd been storing up.

Back in LA: I didn't buy into "The People's World" political line which gravitated toward the Kremlin. Still, it was good to keep in that journalistic flow, writing up reports when I could. My goal living in LA I was to establish residency in California to go to film school at U.C.L.A. Tuition was free for residents; just had to buy your books then. But once I found myself living in LA, though, I realized after almost a year that I just couldn't stand that LA haze any more.

I got turned on to a biography of Jack Kerouac by a friend in Seattle. That inspired me to hit the road. I found a paperback copy of <u>On the Road</u> at a used bookstore in a most unusual, synchronistic way: it was the very first book I pulled off of a shelf; seemed it almost jumped off the shelf, too, into my hands. I went through the entire collection in that large bookstore looking for any more by Kerouac. Not a single book by Kerouac showed up.

So book in hand, pages occasionally flying out of it on the road, I began my journey to Seattle, hitchhiking up California's coast. I camped out for a while in the redwood forests in Northern California to clear my lungs some of that soupy thick LA smog. Then I ended up in Seattle for several months, living next to Lake Washington.

A death in the family, my grandfather's, called me back East to Savannah. I took to the highway, Kerouac style, hitchhiking from Seattle to Savannah, a journey filled with wild rides, especially in Louisiana where just about every driver was either drunk or stoned.

Once back in Savannah, I decided to get into restoration work: first I worked as a carpenter, then a general contractor and restored some 40 historic houses in downtown Savannah. I had gotten married and had a son as well as restored the house we lived in, one I later rented out as a B & B—the St. Julian St. B & B.

Eventually, I returned to Tybee Island where I'd grown up. Divorced, I re-married a Yoga teacher I met at – where else but a Yoga class at the Tybee Y. I took teacher training so that I too could be teaching Yoga. Which is what I've been doing for the past 10 years. That and writing poems which I am happy to finally be publishing.

Will Strong